How to Get a Place on an

Airline Pilot

Training Scheme

Published by

Get That Job! Guides

How to Get a Place on an

Airline Pilot

Training Scheme

A catalogue record is available from the British Library.

ISBN 0 9531837 0 X

First published in 1997 by Get That Job! Guides.

Revised and updated 1998.

We welcome all comments and suggestions, as well as ideas for new titles,
so please feel free to write to us at:

Get That Job! Guides. (01892 870015)
6 Latymers, Penshurst, Tonbridge, Kent, TN11 8DE.

or e-mail us at GetThatJobGuides@btinternet.com

Contents

page

Part 2 - The Selection Process

Part 3 - The Alternatives to Sponsorship

Introduction

The aim of this guide is to give you, the would-be airline pilot, as much help as possible in obtaining your dream job of a place on an airline pilot sponsorship / training scheme. By the end of this guide you should have a good idea of who is likely to be recruiting trainee pilots in the near future and also how to excel through the airline selection process, and thereby gain a head start on fellow candidates.

The first part of this book outlines the many airline pilot training schemes that are now available. The second part tells you how to maximise your chances of getting a place on one of them, and takes you through the selection process. This is your route to the right hand seat (and one day the left) in the cockpit of a major airliner. The third part is a quick look at some alternative ways of learning to fly, including joining one of the services, and my predictions for the future of pilot recruitment and training.

You will find throughout this guide numerous acronyms, abbreviations and maybe the odd term you are not familiar with, so I have put a short glossary of the main ones at the end should you need to refer to it. Although the odd one or two you might have to work out for yourself!

I should point out that the aviation business is constantly changing, and nowhere more so than in the field of pilot recruitment. I have tried as much as possible to make sure that this latest edition is as up to date as it possibly can be, but training costs, entry requirements, salaries and terms and conditions will inevitably change, so please do check with the airlines concerned before you apply.

I would also like to take this opportunity to thank everyone who has helped in the preparation, research and writing of this book, with names too many to mention but you know who you are.

If you have any comments please feel free to drop me a line, or email me at Sam.Maybrey@btinternet.com. I am always especially keen to hear from anyone who has just been through the recruitment process at a particular airline, even if they were unsuccessful, so that I can keep this book up to date. So please keep those e-mails coming, or write to me via the publishers at the address given on the back cover.

I hope you will enjoy reading the following pages and that they help you to realise your ambition of obtaining what is, probably, the best job in the world.

Good Luck!

Sam Maybrey. Get That Job! Guides. December 1997

Part 1

Airline Sponsorship Schemes

There are three well trodden paths to becoming a professional pilot:

- get sponsored by an airline for all or part of the cost of training;

- join the services i.e. RAF, Navy or Army and train as a pilot;

- pay for flying lessons yourself, obtaining a Private Pilots Licence followed by further exams and flying experience necessary to obtain a full commercial jet licence.

This section looks at the first of these as airline sponsorship is not only the best way of getting a job as an airline pilot but also the best way to start your professional flying career.

Airline Sponsorship

Make no mistake, none of the paths to becoming a professional pilot are easy, but it has recently become a great deal easier on account of the fact that the recession in the aviation industry in the early 1990's has now passed. Up until about three years ago there were still significant numbers of qualified pilots without jobs, meaning that none of the airlines were sponsoring trainee cadet pilots. Fortunately this situation has now changed, the market for qualified pilots is generally good and there are airlines willing to sponsor candidates with little or no previous flying experience. What's more, demand for air travel has been increasing significantly just at the same as the supply of qualified pilots from the services has been falling. That's great news for you as it means seeking sponsorship from a major or minor airline (including charter operators) is now a realistic possibility.

You only need to look at the profit figures of the major airlines to see how things are currently shaping up, and who is (and isn't) most likely to be in need of new pilots. For example, during 1996 British Airways was arguably the world's most profitable as well as the world's favourite airline (it does depend how you work out the figures though), making a net profit of $865m. Close behind British Airways was American Airlines ($854m), Singapore Airlines ($731m), Northwest ($536m), and United Airlines ($533m). However, just as fast as some airlines were making money others were busy losing it, including Alitalia with a net loss of ($779m), Swissair ($402m), Sabena ($286m) and TWA ($285m).

So the following is a brief guide to the main sponsorship and training schemes, with details of entry qualifications, numbers recruited and cost where applicable.

British Airways

The major employer of pilots in the UK is obviously British Airways and they have now started once again to run what they call their cadet entry pilot training scheme. This is great news for aspiring pilots as it not only signifies the fact that British Airways need new pilots but it also shows that there is no longer a large number of high quality unemployed pilots still looking for work in the market place. If there were, British Airways would go out and employ them rather than spend huge sums of money training new pilots, assuming of course that any unemployed pilots were of sufficiently high calibre.

The cadet pilot scheme was run again in the autumn of 1995, with a second recruitment campaign during August 1997. Advertisements were run in Flight International, The Sunday Times Appointments Section, The Times Appointments Section (Thursday), Cosmopolitan magazine, Asian Times and The Weekly Journal, as well as within BA itself. You can see by the variety of media used the depths to which BA will now go to try to ensure that women and ethnic minorities are targeted. (Over 90 % of airline pilots are currently male). Prior to that the last time BA ran its own flying school was 1976. If you are thinking about a career as an airline pilot you are very lucky in that the aviation business is currently on a strong upswing - meaning more jobs for pilots. Added to this is the fact that a high percentage of BA pilots will reach retirement age within ten years, meaning that new pilots will have to be trained even if there is no significant increase in air travel.

However, don't worry about watching the press like a hawk and buying every copy of *Flight International* in the hope of seeing an ad, because British Airways have a 24 hour recorded recruitment line giving details of the posts they are currently accepting applications for. It's worth ringing this on a regular basis. The number is 0181 564 1450. Should you actually want to speak to a human being about the scheme you can normally get hold of one of the very polite and usually very helpful people in Flight Operations Recruitment on 0181 564 1422.

So what's on offer?

Basically with the British Airways sponsored cadet pilot scheme BA will train you to fly modern jet aircraft from scratch in about 70 weeks. You don't need any previous flying experience as a pilot (see later) and the course covers every aspect of commercial flying. Successful candidates will gain their Commercial Pilots Licence (and subsequently the ATPL) which is the basic qualification needed to fly passengers for reward.

Once qualified your first job with BA is likely to be as a co-pilot flying twin engined aircraft such as the ATP, Boeing 737 or 757 to destinations throughout Europe. Subsequently you could find yourself flying all over the world as a co-pilot and eventually Captain of aircraft like the Boeing 747 - 400 series and 777, and maybe, just maybe Concorde.

Salaries for pilots within BA are largely linked to seniority which is in turn dependent on length of service rather than aircraft or routes flown. This has the significant advantage of allowing experienced pilots with young families to alternate between long and short haul routes without loss of salary or seniority, enabling staff to spend more time at home when it is necessary.

What does the course involve?

British Airways has chosen the Australian Aviation College Adelaide and Cabair College of Air Training, Cranfield, UK to train its next generation of pilots. The training programme is likely to start off with 8 weeks classroom teaching covering all aspects of aviation theory and practice. Subjects covered include aerodynamics, meteorology, engineering, navigation, radio operation and aviation law.
This is followed by flight training in a single engined two seater aircraft with an instructor, enabling you to obtain your Private Pilots Licence.

You can then move on to larger twin engine aircraft covering aspects such as instrument and night flying. You will also learn how to fly in poor weather and how to work as pilot and co-pilot.

After considerable time spent studying on the ground as well as practising in the air you will be able to begin flying in controlled airspace, and you will be able to sit the CAA Instrument Rating exam. Further simulator training on larger jet aircraft and more exams and flying tests should then result in you gaining your Commercial Pilots Licence.

How much does it cost?

The BA scheme is currently unique in that it does not require you to pay up front for *any* of the cost of training. BA pay for all your tuition, flying, accommodation and examination costs which amount to over £ 60,000 (of which 25% is repayable from salary once you join British Airways. The remainder is non-repayable, provided you remain with the airline for at least five years. This makes it one of the best schemes in the business. (These figures may well change in the future so check direct with BA).

How many people?

British Airways took on around 85 cadet pilots in 1996, and they hope to increase this number up to about 200 per year in a few years time. They then plan to have a continual intake which will probably vary in accordance with how British Airways performs and the cyclical nature of the aviation business. Naturally applicants for the scheme run into thousands, but given the quality of the training, the company and the job on offer the odds aren't too bad.

British Airways Selection Criteria

The following were the selection criteria for the BA cadet scheme as advertised during September 1997. This may well change for future recruitment programmes and this guide will be updated as soon as any changes occur. The British Airways selection criteria should give you a good idea as to what the other airlines will require as well, although BA is generally regarded as tougher than average. Incidentally, you cannot apply for the British Airways scheme if you have applied for it or any other British Airways programme within the last three years - but I shouldn't take this too literally.

Age

Applicants must be between the ages of 18 and 28 at the time of application, but you may be 29 when you start training.

Residency

European Economic Area citizen, eligible for unrestricted world-wide passport.

Academic Ability

7 GCSEs or equivalent at Grade C or above, including English, Maths and a Science subject.
2 or more 'A' Levels at Grade C or above, or equivalent, ideally including Maths or Physics.

Willing to undertake intensive academic study and to sit professional exams. Highly numerate with a head for figures.

Physical Attributes

Height between 1.57m (5'2) and 1.91m (6'3) with weight in proportion to height. Physically fit and able to satisfy CAA and BA medical requirements.

Good hand to eye co-ordination and practical aptitude. Normal vision (wearing glasses does not mean automatic rejection).

Communication Skills

Fluent in English with a clear speaking voice. Confident communication skills. Ability to win the confidence and co-operation of others. Ability to share knowledge and co-operate as part of a team.

Aptitude

Close attention to detail, particularly when working with figures. Analytical and able to understand and apply technical data. Calm under pressure, even when managing a number of tasks simultaneously. Spatial awareness with the ability to interpret maps and 3 dimensional displays. Excellent powers of observation.

Selection Process

Last time this took place at BA offices at Heathrow. The selection process included computer based and written aptitude tests in addition to interview and group activities. Offers are conditional on passing CAA medical and references.

Medical Requirements...

Class 1 Medicals

Before any airline can let you loose on its aircraft and its passengers you need to pass what is known as a Civil Aviation Authority Class 1 Medical. This is the medical requirement for pilots flying paying passengers as opposed to just themselves and maybe a friend as a private pilot. Private pilots need only a Class 3 Medical which is less onerous. So if you are seeking sponsorship you will need to pass the Class 1 Medical with ease before any airline spends their hard earned profits training you, as this sets the *minimum* medical requirements for UK commercial aircrew.

An airline offering sponsorship may seek higher medical standards than those required to pass a Class 1 Medical to allow for some deterioration during your working career.

Generally speaking the more money an airline is investing in your training the tougher the medical standards. So with BA where they are paying for most of the cost of training you should expect it to be tough, but you may find some of the smaller airlines less strict as you will be putting up more of the money. But remember, whoever is paying for your training, even if you pay for it all yourself at a flying school, you must still pass the CAA Class 1 Medical, and what's more pass it again and again throughout your career. This is worth bearing in my mind before you spend your life's savings on flying lessons.

You can obtain further specific details on Class 1 Medical Requirements from the CAA Medical Dept at Gatwick on 01293 573685.

British Airways Medical Requirements

The following should give you some idea as to the medical standards required for British Airways and they are a good indicator of the standards that would be required by other airlines offering sponsorship. However, you should be aware that the ability to achieve these standards will not necessarily ensure acceptability by British Airways.

Applicants are required to be:

- free from any abnormality, congenital or acquired; any active, latent or chronic disability; any wound, injury or sequelae from operations which, in itself or its treatment, may be judged likely to interfere with the safe operation of an aircraft, or which may be aggravated by working in a changing pressure environment and world wide geographical regions;

- free from any established history of psychosis, alcoholism, drug dependence, personality disorder, mental abnormality or neurosis of significant degree;

- not pregnant at time of CAA medical;

- free from hearing defects;

- within height range 5'2 to 6'3 (1.57 to 1.91m) with weight in reasonable proportion*

and should have:

- normal colour perception;

- normal field of vision;

- distant visual acuity of not less than 6/9 in each eye separately, with or without the use of correcting lenses. Where achieved only with correcting lenses, visual acuity in each eye, separately without correction, must not be less than 6/24.* (The CAA rules for a Class 1 Medical state that visual acuity in each eye separately, without correction, must not be less than 6/60.)

* additional British Airways requirement

Before attending final selection tests and interview, applicants will be sent a medical questionnaire and examination form to be completed by their own doctor.

Where doubt exists regarding visual requirements and in any case, if the applicant wears glasses or contact lenses, an optician's report must accompany the above medical questionnaire giving details of:

- field of vision;

- unaided visual acuity;

- corrected visual acuity for spectacles / contact lenses;

- the prescription for spectacles / contact lenses;

- confirmation that contact lenses, if worn, have been worn constantly and successfully for several hours a day over a period of at least three months.

British Airways will not be responsible for the payment of any medical fees at this stage.

Successful applicants are then required to attend a subsequent comprehensive medical examination including physical, x-ray, audiometric and electrocardiographic examinations and should note that extensive blood and urine testing will be carried out for evidence of biochemistry functions, the presence of drugs and sexually transmitted conditions such as HIV (AIDS) antibodies. British Airways will normally be responsible for any costs arising from this medical examination, including the awarding of a CAA Class 1 Medical Certificate.

Applicants who already hold a CAA Class 1 Medical Certificate must have the certificate available for inspection at the time of the medical examination.

Make sure you pass the medical...

In order to minimise the chance of any problems with the medical it may well pay to change your diet a little about a month beforehand, concentrating on reducing your cholesterol level amongst other things. You can also reduce the chance of any trouble with the diabetes test. So cut out fats and sugars as much as you can, eat as much fresh fruit and vegetables as possible and try to cook chicken and fish (but not in oil) instead of red meat. Half fat milk on your bran cereal might be wise too. So I'm afraid you'll have to do without the roast potatoes, double cream and pork scratchings. If you are not particularly fit then take up a mild form of exercise, jogging or cycling for example.

British Midland

British Midland have run a sponsorship programme for the previous two years with Oxford Air Training School, offering basically the same qualification as the British Airways scheme. The scheme was last advertised in October 1996 in Flight International and British Midland were looking for in the region of 16 trainee pilots. They had over 1200 applications, 90% of which, incidentally, were from male applicants. However, if you are female, don't let this put you off as airlines are very keen to recruit female pilots and now apply rigorous monitoring to their selection process to ensure it is not disadvantaging any one category of applicant.

Out of the 1200 or so applications 429 candidates were invited to the testing session (for which the candidates had to pay £50). Out of these 429, 100 or so were interviewed by Oxford Air Training School and then 40 names were passed to British Midland to make the final selection.

British Midland anticipate advertising again in September 1997, most probably in Flight International, for two courses due to commence during 1998. The first of these is likely to start between July and August 1998.

Candidates who have applied in previous years may apply again so long as they have not already been interviewed by British Midland.

Potential candidates who have already passed the Navigation group of subjects at ATPL level or who hold a BCPL or higher level qualification will be considered too experienced for this sponsorship scheme, and therefore should not apply.

Selection Criteria:

- be between the ages of 20 and 28 at the start of the course;

- have at least 5 GCSEs at grade C or above to include Maths, English and a Science subject;

- passes at 'A' Level, preferably Maths and Physics;

- capable of passing a CAA Class 1 Medical;

- some experience of handling light aircraft, whilst not essential, may be an advantage.

- be UK residents for tax purposes and have the unrestricted right to live and work in the UK and be able to obtain a worldwide passport.

Cost

The following outlines the costs relating to the scheme as advertised during October 1996. It is likely that the costs for future schemes will vary, especially relating to the proportion which candidates are expected to pay back to British Midland, as will the precise terms of the arrangement, so check directly with BM at the appropriate time.

If successful at interview and aptitude tests, you are required to pay 25% of the cost of the course before starting and then pay a further 50% back, which is in the form of a 5 year loan, after starting work with British Midland. The total cost to you is in the region of £ 36,000. Last year's successful applicants had to put up a cash sum in the region of £ 13,250 assuming they were eligible for Vocational Training Relief (VTR).

The British Midland scheme is recognised as counting towards a National Vocational Qualification in Piloting Transport Aircraft and as such students who meet the qualifying criteria under the provisions of the 1991 Finance Act are eligible for 23% Vocational Training Relief (i.e. tax relief) on the relevant training fees. You should bear in mind that for every 1% reduction in the basic rate of tax the net outlay increases by approximately £ 174 at current prices. This means that given that the basic rate of tax was 24% when the scheme was advertised last year and that it is now 23% the amount candidates must initially raise will have gone up by £ 174.

In order to qualify for VTR students must be able to sign a declaration which includes the following statements:

"I am resident in the UK for UK tax purposes". This means that the student must be in the UK for at least 183 days in the tax year in which he or she makes the payment on which VTR is claimed. **You do not actually have to be a tax payer.**

"To the best of my knowledge and belief I am not receiving and am not entitled to receive any public financial assistance ... which would prevent my claiming relief for this particular course." The main types of public financial assistance that disqualify a student from claiming VTR are Career Development Loans, Student Loans and mandatory / discretionary local education authority grants, but **only if they are in respect of this course.** Assistance provided for other courses (i.e. university) does not count. The Inland Revenue definition of *entitled to receive* is that a student has been offered the assistance. If you do not apply you will not receive an offer!

Medical Requirements

The medical requirements for the British Midland scheme are very similar to those for British Airways, with the obvious essential requirement that you can easily pass a CAA Class 1 Medical. Unfortunately British Midland aren't quite as generous as British Airways in that before finally selecting you for training they insist that you pay for your own Class 1 Medical at a cost to you of £ 195 - with no certainty of being offered a job. However, at least once you have passed it you will be able to use your medical certificate when you apply to other airlines.

Selection Process

The selection process is similar to the British Airways scheme with aptitude and personality tests followed by interviews with both Oxford Air Training School (who teach the course) and finally British Midland. You might find the initial application form a little less daunting though than the British Airways form as it is shorter with fewer long questions.

Candidates who are successful at the first phase (application form) will be invited to Oxford for a series of occupational tests and responses to written questions taking approximately half a day. A charge of £ 50 will be made to cover administration costs.

Those candidates who are successful at the second phase will be invited to return to the school at a later date for an interview conducted by the school's assessment team. Final selection will be made by British Midland at their headquarters and this will take the form of an interview(s).

Details of the skills and qualities they are looking for and how to get a head start on the other candidates are in the next section.

Classroom Training

This is generally known as ground school and it will help you to have some idea of what subjects are likely to be covered. Afterall, you will spend about 800 hours of classroom time studying these, and considerably more of your own time, so if these subjects don't interest you at all then perhaps airline flying is not for you. These are generally speaking the same whichever airline you land a job with because these subjects form the basis of the UK CAA syllabus for the ATPL ground examinations.

Principles of Flight (Aeroplanes)
Navigation (General & Plotting)
Meteorology (Theory & Practical)
Radio Aids
Flight Planning
Instruments
Engines
Electrics & Automated Flight
Airframe Systems
Loading
Aircraft Performance E & Aircraft Performance Group
Human Performance & Limitations
Aviation Law, Flight Rules & Procedures, Signals

Salary

Assuming you make it through the course and that British Midland
offer you a job once training is completed, you can expect a salary
in the region of £ 19,000 rising to around £ 27,000 once you have
finished repaying the airline after five years. (These figures may of
course change in the future so check direct with British Midland).
After that further pay rises may be obtained through a combination
of promotion and length of service, and your goal should be to reach
the rank of Captain. It is very hard to predict how long this will take
as it can vary hugely between airlines, with factors such as the
aviation cycle, the overall age profile of pilots and your ability all
playing their part. Up until recently it has taken some people in a
variety of airlines up to twenty years to make Captain, but I expect in
the future this period of time will shorten.

Britannia

Britannia have run a sponsored pilot training scheme in the past, but it has not been run recently. However, assuming the strong growth in air travel continues, particularly in the long haul charter market, it is likely that Britannia will run its sponsored scheme again before too long. So watch this space. As with all of the following smaller airlines it is likely that they will advertise their sponsorship schemes in *Flight International, Pilot* or both, so keep an eye on these publications. Reading *Flight International* in particular will also keep you informed as to how the aviation business is performing and it is this that will dictate the need to train new pilots.

The last time the Britannia scheme was advertised the selection criteria were as follows:

- candidates should be not less than 18 and not more than 25 years of age at the commencement of the course;

- candidates should be physically fit and able to pass the CAA Class 1 Medical;

- candidates should have obtained a minimum of 5 GCSE/O Level passes to include English Language, Maths and Physics.

An added but by no means essential criterion would be the possession of or training towards a Private Pilots Licence.

The cost of the course was in the region of £ 45,000. Candidates were required to pay 50% of the cost by an initial deposit of £ 12,000 prior to commencement of the course and by repayment of the remaining 25% over a number of years once the course was successfully completed and employment with Britannia taken up.

Air 2000

Air 2000 advertised their first pilot sponsorship scheme in the October 21st 1997 issue of *Flight International.* They were looking for 12 pilots to be sponsored over a two year period. This just goes to show how much things have improved in the job market for pilots over the last couple of years. Prior to 1997 a relatively small operator such as Air 2000 would have had no trouble sourcing adequately trained pilots from the existing 'pool' of pilots who had either paid for their own training or been trained by other airlines / the services.

The selection criteria are as follows:

- hold a Class 1 Medical;

- hold a minimum of 5 GCSEs at grade C or above;

- hold at least 2 'A' level passes, preferably in science subjects;

- be between the ages of 18 and 28 on 6.3.98.

The first phase of the recruitment process is based upon the application form. Phase two includes a series of written aptitude tests and a short interview to check credentials and suitability at the Cabair College of Air Training, Cranfield. A charge of £47 is made to cover the costs of the day.

Successful candidates are then invited to the third phase of the selection process which includes further mechanical aptitude and psychometric testing of a more practical nature. No previous flying experience is required for any of the tests given. A further interview will probably take place at this stage. A charge of £78 will be made to candidates attending the day in order to cover costs.

Phase four takes place at the offices of Air 2000 at Gatwick Airport, and this will take the form of an extended interview with representatives from the airline. The training course for those selected is expected to start on 6th March 1998, leading to the awarding of a CAA frozen ATPL.

Pilot candidates must be prepared to bind themselves to Air 2000 for a period of five years employment following graduation from the training course and successful completion of type conversion training. Candidates will also have to provide acceptable security by way of a guarantee to the sponsor in respect of all costs repayable to Air 2000 Ltd in the event that the sponsored candidate fails to complete the five years of bonded employment. This is normally in the form of a parental guarantee.

Costs

Air 2000 pays up to £ 26,000 + VAT towards the cost of training, exams, accommodation etc., the balance being met by the candidate. Assuming VAT at 17.5% and NVQ tax relief at 23% the amount payable by the candidate at current prices comes to £ 18,775. Obviously a change in the tax rate will alter this figure (see section on British Midland). Successful applicants will be required to pay their contribution in full by 6th February 1998, one month prior to the commencement of the course.

Salary

On the assumption that employment as a pilot is offered after completing all appropriate training, candidates will be paid the then current salary of other Air 2000 staff of similar qualifications and experience less £ 3,200 per annum sponsorship repayment. This amounts to a total repayment of £ 16,000 over the five year period. A sponsored pilot can therefore expect a starting salary, after sponsorship deduction, in the region of £ 30,000 per annum, although this may be subject to adjustment. No salary is paid whilst candidates are undergoing training.

Air Atlantique

Air Atlantique does occasionally run a sponsorship scheme, the basic requirements of which are as follows:

- be able to pass the CAA commercial pilot written exams;

- hold a UK PPL with approximately 100 hours;

- hold a current British or European passport;

- be under 28 years of age;

- hold a Class 1 Medical;

- be willing to sign an agreement imposing an element of financial repayment for training received in the event of your leaving the company within a specified period;

- be able to fit into the Air Atlantique Group.

KLM / Air UK & Cabair Flying Schools

The sponsorship that KLM / Air UK undertakes for pilots is in conjunction with the Cabair Group of flying schools. This provides financial assistance for PPL holders to obtain AFI, QFI, ATPL (frozen), IR and performance A qualifications during a two year period with the Cabair Group after which those that are selected can join Air UK as first officers. This scheme was last advertised in *Flight International* on 23rd April 1997, and Cabair / Air UK were looking for 12 people to commence training in September 1997 and January 1998.

The entry qualifications are:

- the applicant must be between 18 and 31 years of age;

- the applicant must hold at least 5 GCSEs or equivalent;

- the applicant must already hold a CAA PPL, RT and IMC Rating, 150 hours total flying time of which 95 hours are P1;

- the applicant must hold a Class 1 Medical.

There is a sum of approximately £ 6000 - 7000 (this may vary each year) that the applicant has to contribute towards the sponsorship scheme.

The scheme is unique in that it is effectively a three - way partnership between the candidate, Cabair Flying Schools and Air UK. The scheme was first run in 1989 with Britannia Airways. The Cabair Group were desperate for flying instructors for all of their seven flying schools as the improving job market for pilots meant that their instructors could get jobs with the airlines, and Britannia knew that it would soon have a need for some new entry-level co-pilots.

Initially candidates are trained at the Cabair College of Air Training, Cranfield in order to get their Basic Commercial Pilots Licence. Further training then gives candidates their instructor's rating enabling them to be employed by the Cabair group as a PPL instructor - on a slightly reduced 'sponsorship' salary of course.

After two years with Cabair the student can then go back to Cranfield in order to get an instrument rating and the required amount of navigation flying for the ATPL as well as carrying out the ATPL flying test. At this point the airline can 'take delivery' of its new employee, who should by now have over 1000 hours, and 'type' training can begin on the aircraft which the successful pilot will commence flying. All in all a great scheme.

The Cabair group of flying schools carry out the initial screening, aptitude tests and interviews, and currently Air UK makes the final decision at its own interview. Aptitude tests include a psychometric questionnaire, a 30 minute general handling test and a 30 minute simulator test of instrument flying ability and instructor potential. The Cabair interview, if you are lucky enough to reach this stage, then covers personal attitudes and aviation knowledge.

Naturally the aptitude tests and interview questions will be substantially different from those where no previous flying experience is required. The interviewers for the Cabair scheme will expect you to have picked up some basic skills and knowledge already, given that you should have 150 hours flying experience at the time of application.

It is actually easier than you might at first think to become a PPL flying instructor and build your flying hours towards the amount required for an ATPL. Currently, once you have 150 hours and an IMC rating you can take your instructor's rating and then be paid to instruct other students. However, from 1st July 1999 under new rules brought in by the Joint Aviation Regulations for Flightcrew Licensing (JAR FCL) only pilots with a Commercial Pilot's Licence can be paid to instruct. All will not be lost, because it will then be possible to obtain a Commercial Pilot's Licence with only 200 hours compared with the previous 700 hours, but 25 hours and the final handling test will have to be completed under instruction at an approved flying college.

Remember, though, that a Basic Commercial Pilot's Licence is only one step towards an ATPL (Airline Transport Pilot's Licence).

Jersey European

Jersey European have recently started a small sponsorship scheme, taking on four trainee pilots. They have not yet decided whether this scheme will be run again, but if so it will be advertised in the aviation press, like the other schemes. Jersey European use the Cabair College of Air Training, Cranfield, and their scheme is a combination of Airline / self sponsorship.

The minimum qualifications for acceptance onto the scheme are 8 GCSE and 2 A Level passes, capable of holding a Class 1 Medical and to be aged between 18 and 28 at the commencement of the course.

Airworld

Airworld does not currently have a sponsorship scheme, but it is intending to do in the future should current market conditions continue. Currently new pilots must have 1500 hours with some jet / heavy turbo-prop experience. However, this may well change, so keep an eye out in the press.

British World Airlines

British World Airlines last advertised for their pilot sponsorship scheme on September 2nd 1997 in Flight International. Successful candidates will be employed by BWA in ground operations for one year prior to joining the flying course. This is seen as a very good foundation for future pilots by the airline. Upon completion of the course to the required standard and after taking into account the commercial needs of the airline, candidates will be offered a position as a First Officer based at London Stansted and / or Aberdeen airports. BWA currently operate Viscount, 146, BAC1-11, ATP and ATR aircraft. No prior flying experience is required and the basic entry qualifications are:

- be capable of holding a Class 1 medical (preference will be given to those people who have already taken steps to obtain one - at their own expense);

- have a minimum of 5 GCSEs and 2 'A' level passes;

- be aged between 18 and 28 at 09.01.98.

The airline pays for half of the cost of training and successful candidates earn their CPL/IR and ATPL over 56 weeks. The course is run at the Cabair College of Air Training, Cranfield. Obviously students have to raise the other half of the cost of training, but this should attract NVQ tax relief.

The selection process is split into four phases. Phase 1 is based upon the completed application form which you must complete in your own handwriting (see later section on how to fill in application forms).

Phase 2 consists of a series of written aptitude tests and a short interview to check credentials at the Cabair College of Air Training, Cranfield. There will be a charge for attending these tests to cover administration costs and this is currently £ 46.87, though of course this may change in the future, so please do check direct with British World / Cabair.

Successful candidates will then be invited back to attend further mechanical aptitude and psychometric testing. No previous flying experience is required for these tests. Another interview is likely to take place at this stage, and a charge of £ 100 will be made to cover the cost of the day. If you don't like the thought of paying more money you can take some consolation from the fact that neither will the other candidates. This should mean that anyone who is not

100% committed will drop out at this stage, meaning less competition for you.

Candidates who are successful at stage three will be invited to the offices of British World Airlines at Southend Airport for an extended interview. Those who are successful at this stage can then expect to start work in an Operations position based at Southend Airport for up to 12 months, prior to starting the residential flying course in January 1999.

Successful candidates will have to enter into a contract with British World Airlines binding them to the airline for a period of six years and month.

This period is made up as follows:

- 13 month training course at Cabair College of Air Training;

- 5 Years bonded employment (including three month induction course).

Cost

Successful candidates will receive sponsorship from British World Airlines in the form of a payment of £ 19,800 + VAT towards approximately half the cost of training, examination and accommodation expenses. The balance will be met by the candidate. Pilot candidates will be required to provide security or guarantees in case the pilot fails to complete the five years of employment with BWA. Most candidates supply parental guarantees if they have no other form of security.

All candidates accepted onto the course will pay the sum of £ 25,773.61 (check with BWA as this may well change). This is inclusive of VAT and tax relief at 23%.

However, you should be aware that British World Airlines does not guarantee to offer you employment as a pilot once you have successfully completed the flying course. Obviously if they had no intention of doing so they would not be running this programme, but you should note the following:

'In the event that employment is not offered immediately following the completion of the course, but that the airline intends to make that offer, pilot graduates will be required to accept the offer for a period up to 3 years following graduation, or to repay all monies advanced by the airline in respect of that training.'

Salary

A salary will be paid whilst the candidate is working within operations prior to joining the flying course, but not once the candidate is on the flying course. Assuming an offer of employment is made having completed the flying course, a salary will be payable although this will be at a lower rate than prevailing market rates for non-sponsored pilots. If you are lucky enough to get this far I would enquire what that salary is likely to be, as it needs to be enough to live on given that you are bound to work for the company for five years.

Monarch Airlines

Monarch have unfortunately decided to cease sponsoring trainee pilots. However on the rare occasions that they employ non type-rated pilots they require an ATPL and a minimum of 2500 hours which must include 500 jet (over 25T) experience.

Airtours

Airtours have recently run a sponsorship scheme but it is currently only available to full-time permanent employees of the company, and it is likely to be some time before it is offered to non-employees. All other new pilots are required to have an ATPL and a minimum of 1500 hours flying time on modern passenger aircraft such as ATP or ATR 42.

Caledonian Airways

Caledonian run a part-sponsorship scheme in conjunction with the Cabair College of Air Training, Cranfield. The scheme was advertised in *Flight International* on 14th May 1997, and over two thousand applications were received. The airline will pay approximately half of the course fees, and successful candidates will start work with Caledonian Airways in the autumn of 1998. Entry qualifications are that you must be between 18 and 35 at 1/8/97, have at least 7 GCSEs or equivalent and 2 'A' Levels or equivalent as well as a Class 1 Medical.

Caledonian flies a mix of Airbus A320, Tristar and DC10 aircraft and is particularly strong in the long haul charter market to destinations including the US, Kenya, Goa and the Maldives.

Aurigny Air Services

Aurigny is a small airline and most of their operations are single crew. Pilots must have 1500 hours PIC on multi-engined aircraft. They have one aircraft which carriers a first officer and this is a Shorts 360. Given their size, I expect sponsorship to be unlikely for the foreseeable future.

Channel Express

All candidates must hold a current British CPL/IR (Frozen ATPL) and have passed the Performance A exam. Thereafter, evidence that the candidate will make an easy transition from the training or general aviation environment to professional airline flying will be sought. In their experience, candidates with experience of operating multi-crew aircraft make the transition easiest.

The accumulation of flying hours is not necessarily an important factor; the quality of the experience is more important than the quantity. A CV from a low-hour pilot but with experience of LOFT (Line Oriented Flying Training) and CRM (Cockpit Resource Management) gained through an approved training course as well as some experience of airways flying around Europe is likely to attract more attention than a CV from a pilot with 2000 hours flying instructor experience at a club.

Unfortunately, no current sponsorships, but watch this space.

Virgin Atlantic

Virgin Atlantic's popularity means that there are many qualified pilots who would like to work for the company, so it does not need to train new ones from scratch. In recent years Virgin has relied on taking some retired British Airways pilots who at the moment have to retire at 55 years of age. I understand British Airways is currently reviewing this policy and is considering extending their pilots' working career up to age 60. Some people at BA are annoyed as a matter of principle that BA is effectively paying for the training of Virgin's pilots too. Virgin also tends to pay people slightly less than other airlines, but many people feel that the atmosphere more than makes up for it. However, it is expanding rapidly, with new routes being added all the time, so don't give up hope. Virgin Atlantic currently has eight 747s and six A340s.

Airlines Based Outside the United Kingdom

Lufthansa Flight Training School - Verkehrsfliegerschule

Lufthansa is one of the very few airlines in the world to run its own flight training school, training pilots not just for Lufthansa itself but for other airlines as well. Since January 1st 1997 Lufthansa Flight Training GmbH (LFT) has been an independent company, although still a subsidiary of Lufthansa German Airlines.

Since its foundation over 40 years ago Lufthansa Flight Training has trained nearly 5000 pilots at its school in Bremen, Germany. Combined with other LFT centres in Frankfurt and Arizona the school has an impressive list of simulators and aircraft. The company also carries out safety training for cabin crew on behalf of other major airlines, as well as Human Factors Training and Emergency Training.

LFT is now one of the first pilot schools to respond to the new requirements stipulated for the European licence. Once this comes into force in 1999 it should make it easier for pilots trained in one European country (to the new licence standard) to gain employment with an airline based in another EC country. This now means that LFT is prepared to take individuals from different member countries and train them to the new standard. Previously this was not possible on account of the complexities of having to adapt the training course to suit the requirements of the aviation authority in each member country. Thus previously the courses were restricted to entrants from Lufthansa or other operators, notably Iberia, Swissair and Air Malta.

However, other clients of LFT in the past have also included Air Canada, Air France, Air Zimbabwe, Airbus Industrie, Alitalia, The Civil Aviation Authority, Czech Airlines, Garuda Indonesia, Gulf Air, Kenya Airways, Kuwait Airways, South African Airways, United Airlines and Virgin Atlantic to name but a few.

Note:

Training with LFT does not necessarily secure placement in a Lufthansa cockpit. At present, Lufthansa is not hiring and has no need for cockpit staff. Students from the ab initio scheme have been employed directly by Lufthansa in the past, and it is possible that the best may be employed by Lufthansa at some point in the future when the airline requires new pilots.

Lufthansa Flight Training Selection Criteria:

- Intermediate school leaving certificate;

- Command of spoken and written English;

- EU national, permanent residency or unrestricted work permit in Germany and possession of unrestricted worldwide passport;

- Successful completion of pre-selection test;

- Flight fitness to Class 1 Medical Standard;

- Visual acuity adjustment may not exceed +/- 3 dioptres; LFT recommend that the medical examination is conducted by the Lufthansa Medical Service in Frankfurt (tel: 0049 69 696 2203), Munich (tel: 0049 89 977 5200), or Hamburg (tel: 00 49 40 5070 2081);

- Minimum age 19. Minimum age for issuance of a licence by the German Federal Aviation Agency is 21;

- LFT advise that any compulsory military or national service is completed before attending the course.

Pre-Selection Test

Prior to commencement of training at the Lufthansa Pilot School in Bremen, applicants must undergo a pre-selection test. This is designed to check your own interest and to determine whether a pilot's career really suits you and so justify your investment in a training course. (For more information on selection, aptitude and personality tests see part two.)

Applications may be submitted at any time, there are no deadlines. After evaluation of your application forms, you will be invited to a pre-selection test which is held weekly, beginning in the autumn of 1997.

At the one day selection event applicants are required to undergo tests in the following areas:

- English proficiency;

- Basic technical knowledge (of simple systems), electrical engineering, mechanics, thermodynamics and fluid dynamics, wave theory;

- Technical understanding of the functioning of simple systems and equipment;

- Mathematics (arithmetic, algebra and geometry);

- Sensomotoric co-ordination in multiple stress situations.

Applicants must pass this pre-selection test in order to qualify for admittance to a training course at the Lufthansa Pilot School. The cost of attending the selection event is currently 300 Deutsch Marks. The pre-selection test can be repeated.

Training Programme

The training course lasts 22 months, the content of which is based upon the future requirements for attaining a European licence.

Instruction will be given in either German and English or English only depending on the language knowledge of the participants.

The course consists of four phases:

• Theoretical tuition and practical training in the USA;

• Theoretical tuition in Bremen;

• Practical training in the USA;

• Theoretical tuition and practical training in Bremen.

Stage one lasts approximately two and a half months, stage two lasts seven months, stage three lasts four months and stage four lasts seven months.

An ongoing quality assurance system throughout the course ensures that applicants are optimally prepared for each subsequent stage in their training.

The first phase of about two and a half months training for an American Private Pilots Licence is designed to provide applicants with confirmation as to whether or not they have chosen the right career. It also helps the LFT instructors to assess an applicant's ability to continue training for an ATPL (Airline Transport Pilot Licence).

Training Cost

The course costs approximately DM 127,500, plus ancillary costs of approx. DM 17,000.

The latter costs include all expenses for teaching material, tests and licence, accommodation in the USA and 2 tickets to the USA. They do not include living expenses, accommodation in Bremen or health insurance.

Financing the Course

No sponsorship will be available from Lufthansa.   Every successful applicant will be expected to finance the full cost of the course him or herself.

Timescale

The courses begin at two-monthly intervals. The first is likely to be held exclusively in English and to start at the end of 1997. Courses cannot be joined mid-way by holders of PPL/A or CPL/IFR.

The Lufthansa scheme looks like a good one, but before you part with what is going to be a large amount of money, I would ask them some searching questions regarding the up to date employment situation of the course's recent graduates. You must also remember that although LFT is a good name to have on your CV they are not sponsoring you and they are not likely to employ you on graduation either. However, they do claim to have many airline contacts to help you find work on graduation, and this should certainly give you a head start in you search for employment. Just watch out for the signs of a down-turn in the aviation business as that is when not being sponsored directly by an employer will be bad news for the low experience pilot job hunter.

For the LFT address and phone numbers see *Airline Addresses* at the end of this book.

South African Airways

South African Airways do currently run a cadet pilot training scheme, taking on approximately 12 cadet pilots every year. The scheme is advertised in national and regional papers within South Africa.

Like the rest of South Africa, SAA is undergoing considerable change with the ending of the apartheid system. To say that SAA is now keen to recruit black people would probably be an understatement. The following quote reflects current policy:

'While the group of cadet pilots will be wholly representative of South Africa's diverse population, the main focus is to open doors to a career that was historically closed to black people.'

SAA knows that in being the country's national airline it has a very high international profile, and must therefore be seen to be recruiting fairly from all sections of the community.

The basic requirements for selection are as follows:

- to be a South African citizen;

- aged between 18 and 25;

- fluent in English;

- at least 1.63m tall and medically fit;

- prepared to undergo vigorous training (free of charge) for up to 2 years;

- prepared to sign a training bond;

- not in possession of a criminal record;

- in possession of a South African Matric certificate and Maths in matric (E Symbol on higher grade or D symbol on standard grade).

Selection Process

The SAA selection process consists of 7 phases. These are:

- pre-screening on application;

- psychometric testing;

- medical examination (equates to PPL Level Medical);

- assessment and clinical interview;

- final medical exam (equates to Class 1 Medical);

- Flight Grading, carried out at 43 Air School, Port Alfred by SAA Instructors;

- final interview.

Candidates must pass each stage of the selection process before going on to the next stage. Phase 1 is a pre-screening of basic requirements. The psychometric phase assesses basic aptitude, i.e. mental alertness, spatial reasoning, English proficiency, arithmetic and reasoning ability (cognitive intuitive behaviour). The first medical is a PPL medical. The assessment phase and clinical interview assess candidates cognitive intelligence, cognitive perception, cognitive intuitive behaviour, self management abilities, communication and interpersonal skills, motivation, confidence and co-ordination.

A variety of techniques are used including individual tests, group exercises, co-ordination tests and simulation exercises. The final medical is the airline pilot medical. A flight grading is carried out to assess basic flying aptitude.

At the final interview candidates are assessed on communication abilities, confidence, decision making, technical knowledge, airline knowledge, command potential, achievement orientation and discipline.

Experience of light aircraft is not an advantage throughout the SAA selection process.

Successful candidates do not have to finance any of the cost of training themselves (this would disadvantage black candidates) and must only repay training costs if SAA offers them a position which they turn down. If SAA chooses not to employ a candidate once training is successfully completed then the candidate is free to seek employment with other airlines and does not have to repay any costs.

The Training Programme

The SAA cadet pilot training scheme takes slightly longer to complete than, for example, the BA scheme. Phase 1 which takes place in South Africa lasts about five and a half months and consists of 8 modules covering the following:

- Maths, physics and computer training;

- Aviation related geography;

- Corporate training;

- Technical training (Avionics, Mechanics, Electronics etc.);

- Aeroplane weight and balance and performance;

- Radio procedural training;

- PPL Theory;

- Drivers Licence - for cadets without a driving licence.

Phase 2 lasts approximately 18 months and takes place at the Australian Aviation College in Adelaide, Australia. Flight training will include 210 flying hours and 45 simulator hours, in addition to 1500 hours ground school. Successful completion will result in a South African commercial pilots licence with Instrument Rating and a frozen ATPL.

Phase 3 involves successful candidates working as cadet first officers with SA Airlink and SA Express with whom SAA have a training agreement. Candidates will work for approximately 2 years building hours on the Dash 8 or Jetstream J41 after which time they will be eligible to join SAA with approximately 1200 hours, subject to successfully passing the SAA selection board.

Successful candidates will then join SAA as first officers on either the B737, A300 or A320. A typical career path would be B737, A300 or A320 and then B747 as co-pilot, then back to B737, A300 or A320 as captain. Currently within SAA it takes approximately 12 years to make Captain.

Salary

Once qualified candidates will start on a salary of roughly
R 60,000 pa. This may not sound much once converted into sterling
(£ 8,000 pa) but that goes a long way in South Africa and you do not
have to pay back any of the training cost.

SAA do also take on qualified pilots from smaller airlines and the
airforce. The minimum requirement is 1000 hours and an
Instrument Rating. Remember too that citizenship / work permit
requirements will need to be satisfied for all jobs based in South
Africa.

Airlines Based in the United States

The aviation business in the US is somewhat different to ours in that there are a much larger number of smaller domestic operators than in the UK on account of distances being so much greater. This means that the really big international American airlines can source a large number of the pilots they need already trained from the national operators without too much trouble. Obviously pilots have got to be trained by someone, and this tends to be a combination of the smaller operators, military and self-sponsorship, with more advanced jet training carried out by the bigger airlines when they take on new staff. However, America is a huge employer of pilots with many 'smaller' US airlines employing more pilots than some European international airlines, so the training situation could well change if the US economy continues its current strong growth.

Using a small private plane in some parts of the US and for some journeys is an essential mode of transport, again due in part to the large distances. Obtaining a PPL in the States is also a great deal cheaper than in the UK and so both of these factors mean that a much higher percentage of people have a PPL than in the UK. Therefore when looking for trainees the airlines of all sizes can often find people who have the potential to make good pilots and who have at least a little flying experience.

However, some of the majors are addressing predictions of a future pilot shortage. United has a large training centre in Denver, Colorado, where pilots are trained for United as well as other airlines. Northwest Airlines has a link up with the University of North Dakota at Grand Forks. An ab initio programme is run here and candidates without college degrees can study for a degree at the same time.

It should also be noted that college degrees are of much greater importance in the US when it comes to getting a pilot job than they *currently* are in the UK. (As time goes on I am sure university degrees will become more important for UK pilots too as educational standards increase for everyone.) So if you're goal is employment as an airline pilot with one of the bigger US airlines I would go for that college degree first if you get the opportunity.

Last of all, for most EC citizens the biggest stumbling block to employment in the US will be a Green Card or work permit. These are not easily obtainable and would only become so for *qualified* pilots were there to be a severe shortage of US qualified pilots. If you are really interested in the US job market the best places to look are in the US flying magazines or on the internet at www.airapps.com. Here you'll find a wide range of specialist books and information on the US pilot job market, with everything from salary surveys to pilot CV preparation services.

United Airlines

United is the world's largest airline, operating more than 2200 daily flights with an aircrew staff of nearly 28,000. United do not operate a cadet pilot sponsorship scheme as such. However, they anticipate recruiting approximately 1000 pilots with varying degrees of experience during 1997, and 500 - 600 during 1998 and 300 per year thereafter.

Salaries are amongst the best in the business with new entrants starting on circa US $26,000, rising to a maximum of $200,000 per year as a Captain on their larger aircraft.

American Airlines

American is one of the world's largest carriers, serving 164 cities. Unfortunately American does not recruit pilots from within Europe as, just like with United Airlines, you would need to be either an

American citizen or possess a Green Card in order to be able to work in the US.

Northwest Airlines

Northwest Airlines has hired over 1000 pilots in the last three years and anticipates continuing to hire 300-400 a year in the next few years. The vast majority of 'new hires' come from either the military or regional airlines with thousands of hours of flying experience.

Northwest Airlines requires that all pilots have a First Class medical with 20/40 minimum vision, correctable to 20/20. Many other airlines in the US also do not require 20/20 vision, and allow the wearing of corrective lenses to restore 20/20 sight.

End of Part 1

The above is by no means intended to be an encyclopaedic guide covering every airline and training scheme. It is merely to give you some idea as to how things are in the market place at the moment and what the basic qualifications are that are necessary to be considered for most schemes. There is a much more comprehensive list of names and addresses at the end which you may find useful when hunting down a potential sponsor, and some of the larger European airlines might well be worth a try if you can speak another language. So long as your employer is based within the EC you won't have any work permit problems either.

Part 2

So How Do I Get In?

In order to make the best possible attempt at gaining a place on any airline sponsorship scheme it helps to have a clear understanding of what the airlines are looking for in potential pilots and what skills and attributes will help new recruits in their flying careers. This should help you to decide for yourself whether you are likely to be good at the job and help you to excel through the selection process by demonstrating the necessary skills.

So the following is a list of the core aptitudes (also known as competencies) airlines will be looking for in potential recruits.

What Qualities are Airlines Looking for in Cadet Entry Pilots?

Basic (flying) handling skills

You must have the potential handling skills to make a good pilot. These will be tested through a number of different aptitude tests, including hand-eye co-ordination and manual dexterity. A computer based assessment may also be used - see section on aptitude tests.

Hand-eye co-ordination

This is very important as it will influence all your key flying skills. You need to be able to co-ordinate successfully what your eyes are telling you and how your mind and body react.

Numeracy and mental agility

Safe flight involves a great deal of number work, from flight planning and navigation, to take-off speeds and weights, altitudes and interrogating the multitude of numerical information available to you in the cockpit.

Motivation

You must *really, really,* want to be an airline pilot more than anything else in order to overcome the significant obstacles and set-backs that you will face along the way. Your potential employer will be looking for evidence of this commitment during the selection process. They do not want you to drop out half way through training once they have spent £ 20,000 training you!

Leadership potential

Despite the fact that modern cockpit teams usually only consist of two people leadership potential is an essential core attribute of any professional pilot. Your employer will be looking to train you to one day take charge of tens of millions of pounds worth of aircraft, and the lives of hundreds of people, so you will need to be the kind of person who is decisive under pressure and gives clear instructions to other members of the crew. You will need the respect of the crew too to make a good Captain, and know how to get the best out of people. Your employer may also be looking for some teaching ability, when it comes to training new pilots and testing existing ones.

There is little room in most airlines for 'career' first officers, i.e. people who for one reason or another do not have the necessary skills and abilities to make Captain. A potential employer will therefore be looking throughout the selection process for evidence that you have the *potential* to one day be a Captain of one of their aircraft. You will also need to demonstrate to them that this is one of your main ambitions.

Ability to work as part of a small team

The two man (or woman) cockpit crew must work efficiently together as a small team, co-operating fully. The flightdeck is not a place for conflict.

Ability to concentrate and not be easily distracted

You will often have to complete several tasks almost simultaneously, and sometimes with a great deal of noise or unexpected things happening in the background.

Critical thinking

The ability to interrogate data in order to ascertain its validity. You should not be fooled by misleading information.

Interest in the business side of air transport

Airlines are businesses in which pilots play one small part. An interest in the business itself will help you understand how it all fits together.

Commitment to the customer

Today the most important person in any airline is the customer, not the chief pilot.

Ability to fit into the airline's business culture

All airlines have certain ways of working and you must be able to adapt easily to these and 'fit in'.

Able to adapt to changing sleep patterns, time zones, climates and cultures

You will not always be home in time for dinner!

Physical fitness

You must be in good physical shape to cope with the physical pressures of flying and the unsettling lifestyle.

Communication skills

You need to be able to communicate well with the rest of the crew, your passengers and other airline / airport staff in order to get the best out of people.

Ability to get on with a wide range of people

Including foreign airport staff and passengers.

Computer literacy

Particularly important these days with modern fly by wire aircraft and 'glass cockpits' where information is often only displayed on a need to know basis.

Fluent, clear English

You must be able to communicate fluently in English with a clear voice.

Most of these core skills will be relevant whichever airline you are applying to. Airlines are increasingly looking for people who will not only be very technically competent in the basic flying skills required to pilot the aircraft but also people who have some understanding of and interest in the wider business issues of air transport. Therefore things like customer service, communication skills and business awareness will all be highly regarded as well. You will be able to increase your awareness of these areas by reading some of the trade press, such as *Flight International*.

British Airways say that for their scheme, in addition to good basic handling, skills your motivation and ability to work as part of a team are crucial. Again this is likely to be true for the other sponsored training schemes such as British Midland.

How to Fill in the Application Form

Before you get anywhere near selection centres or interviews - let alone runways, airports or aeroplanes - you will have to successfully complete the application form. This can be quite a task in itself, especially the British Airways form as there are usually several quite taxing questions followed by large blank spaces for your answer.

The key to application forms is don't rush them. Take time to read through the *whole* form before you write *anything*. Treat them rather like exams except without the time pressure. If you haven't filled in many application forms it is probably a good idea to photocopy it first and write it all out in rough, checking your spelling and making sure your answers fit nicely into the spaces provided. The only danger with this is that it is easy to make a small mistake when copying out the final version, so be *very* careful when you write the final version as you will only get one chance to get it right.

Read all the questions and think about what answers you could give, bearing in mind what the other questions are as it is better not to keep using the same examples to demonstrate different skills. The more difficult questions will usually be scenario type questions in which you have to explain how you handled a particular situation and what you learnt. Generally the reader is going to be looking at the following in your answers so bear these in mind:

- how did you decide what to do?

- what did you do?

- how did you do it?

- what motivated you to do it?

- how did you interact with others?

- did you need to motivate or organise others? If so how did you do it?

- did you discuss the plan of action as a group and come to a joint decision? If so *how* did you arrive at a decision when some of you disagreed?

- what *specifically* did *you* do? - try *not* to generalise or talk about what you *could* have done;

- what did you learn?

- what was the outcome?

Don't worry too much if you don't seem to have lots of really good examples of the type of thing they're after, especially if you are a younger applicant. If you think hard enough there are bound to be things you can use. For example, when you played in the school or university sports team, or when you went on a French exchange holiday, or maybe even when you went hiking, got lost, and had to call out mountain rescue!

Remember the key is to give specific examples of what you did and how you did it, with the emphasis on your role if you were working as a group. Incidentally, if the cadet pilot scheme for BA is not currently open when you are reading this and you want an idea of the *type* of questions found on previous cadet pilot training programme application forms get hold of the current BA graduate application form. You can do this by ringing graduate recruitment on 0181 564 1367 - or ring the recorded message recruitment line on 0181 564 1450 to see if the scheme is open. You'll find that many of the questions are very similar to those that I have given in the section on interview questions which follows later, so look at these too to get a feel for the type of question you will need to answer.

The person who ends up reading your application form will be desperately looking for reasons to put it in the 'definitely invite for aptitude testing' pile, so try to give him or her those reasons, preferably on the first page. So try to do the following:

- make your form look good especially on the first page as first impressions really count;

- write clearly and neatly;

- make sure your spelling is 100%;

- check that your answers are in sentences;

- make sure your answers fill the gaps neatly, but don't waffle just to use up space;

- make sure you answer the question - and not the one you thought you read or would like to answer;

- try to send your form back as soon as possible and not right on the deadline;

- make the most of your achievements, and be positive;

- don't lie, but don't volunteer negative information either;

- finally, before you send off your immaculate application form, photocopy it so that you will be able to refresh your memory of what you said before you go to an interview.

Selection and Aptitude Tests

Whichever airline sponsorship schemes you apply for you are likely to be faced with aptitude tests. In order to get ahead of the competition it is a good idea to have had a little practice at some of things you might find, especially if you have not recently done much work involving mental arithmetic. Likely tests include numerical and verbal reasoning, spatial and diagrammatic reasoning and various tests assessing hand-eye co-ordination. You may also get basic 'checking' tests in which you have to match one line of figures or letters with another, usually no more than seven characters at a time. There are several good books that can help you in this regard and these are:

How to Pass Technical Selection Tests, Bryon and Modha, 1993;

How to Pass the Civil Service Qualifying Tests, Bryon 1995;

How to Pass Computer Selection Tests, Sanjay Modha, 1994;

How to Pass Graduate Recruitment Tests, Mike Bryon, 1994;

How to Pass Selection Tests, Mike Bryon and Sanjay Modha, 1991;

How to Win at Aptitude Tests, Paul Pelshenke, 1993.

These are all published by Kogan Page except the last one which is published by Thorsons. All of these books have examples of some of the types of exercise that you might be given. You can also look on the internet at www.airapps.com for specific books on airline aptitude tests amongst other things. However, bear in mind that they will all be based on the American aviation industry as the company is based in Atlanta, USA.

So whichever book you get practice working through some of the questions under time pressure. Speed and accuracy are the key, and you will find the real tests are hard to complete in the time given. I would normally advise against guessing since this will drastically reduce your accuracy figure and you cannot be sure on what basis your results will be assessed.

You can also apply for a job as an Air Traffic Controller and sit their selection tests just for practice, as some of their tests are quite similar to those used by the airlines. This may help in particular with any diagrammatic and spatial tests, as examples of these can be harder to find. It is also just good to practice working quickly and under pressure at these types of test. Given the level of competition for pilot training schemes this might just make the difference between getting through to the next round and not doing so. ATC usually send out sample questions prior to the testing session and you can use these for practice too.

Examples of hand-eye co-ordination tests may also be harder to find as they are more specific to the aviation industry. However, common exercises include drawing a line quickly between two other lines, drawing ticks very quickly in a large number of boxes and joining up dot to dots quickly and accurately. Some airlines are now using more advanced computer based tests, but the principles and skills they are looking for are similar.

Numeracy is obviously very important and this is much easier to practice. Learning the following might be useful too as they often come up in number pattern tests:

- the decimal equivalent of fractions down to about 1/16, 1/2, 1/3, 1/4, 1/5, 1/6, 1/7, etc.

- squares of numbers, i.e. 1, 4, 9, 16, 25, 36, 49, 64, etc.

- cubes of numbers, i.e. 1, 8, 27, 64, 125, 216, 343, 512.

You'll find lots of tests to practice numerical and verbal reasoning skills in the books I've mentioned above, but pay particular attention to the numerical sequence questions as these are very common.

With a bit of practice you'll be able to spot many of the patterns straight away.

Interviews

Interviews are an entire subject in themselves, but if you are lucky enough to get through to this stage you again need to be thinking in terms of the skills and attributes that the airlines are looking for. Your motivation and team abilities are likely to be under heavy scrutiny as are your extra-curricular activities, business awareness, commitment and strengths and weaknesses.

So read through the copy of your application form that you made before you sent it off and be prepared to expand on your answers. If you haven't been for any interviews recently - or at all for that matter - try to get some practice before hand, maybe with parents or a neighbour.

The following is a list of the sort of questions you might be asked, so try to think how you might answer them and try to anticipate any follow-up questions to your answers. The key is to know what you are going to say to most of the more obvious questions without your answers sounding as if you are reading off of a script that you have learnt. Most important of all is to put across your enthusiasm for the job, the company and the training being offered.

Interview Questions

Why do you want to be an airline pilot?

Why do you think you would make a good pilot?

Why should we employ you and not the next candidate?

What other careers are you considering? Why?

Have you had any other interviews recently? If so where? What was the outcome?

Why do you want to work for Snappy Airlines as opposed to any other?

What routes do Snappy Airlines fly?

What aircraft do we use? What do you know about them?

Who is the Chief Executive at Snappy?

How would you describe the aviation business at the moment?

How has our share price performed recently? Why do you think this is?

What challenges do you think Snappy will face in the future?

How do you think we should approach these?

How do you feel about reducing the cost base of the airline?

What do you think should determine pilots' salaries?

Who is the most important person in an airline?

How did you choose what subjects to study at 'A' Level?

With hindsight was this the correct choice?

Describe a situation when you have worked as a member of a team.

What were the team's goals? How were these goals set?

Who had most influence over deciding what action the team should take? Why?

Did the team have a natural leader or was one appointed?

What was your role in the team?

Did you seek this position or were you just appointed?

Was this a role you enjoyed or would you have rather done something different?

If you would have preferred a different role did you make your views known?

If so how did the team react? Were you able to change their minds?

Did the team achieve its goals? What did the team learn from this?

What did you learn?

What would you have done differently faced with the same set of circumstances?

Describe a situation where you have changed someone's point of view.

Why did you want to do this?

How did you go about it?

What was their reaction?

What was the outcome?

Describe a situation in which you have followed a set of rules or instructions.

Did you find this easy?

Did you feel some of the instructions or rules were unnecessary?

If so did you still carry them out?

Give an example of a situation when you have ignored an instruction or broken a rule.

What was the outcome?

What motivates you?

Give an example of when you have overcome obstacles and / or setbacks to achieve a goal.

Describe a situation when you have explained something complicated to a group of people.

How did you go about this?

How did they react? What was the outcome?

Describe a situation when you have led a team or group.

How did you motivate yourself and the team?

What was their reaction? What was the outcome? What did you learn?

What sports do you play? Why?

Are you good at them?

Is always winning important to you?

Give an example of a situation where you have admitted to being wrong.

Why did you admit to being wrong?

Did you find this difficult?

When have you worked with people from different backgrounds?

Did you find this easy? How were they different?

Have you ever taken drugs?

Have you ever been sued?

Do you have any debts?

Do you own a house?

Did you like school / university?

What will you do if you don't get this job?

Have you applied to the forces? If not why not?

What do you like best / least about flying?

What do you think your best / worst qualities are?

So think through *why* you really want to be an airline pilot, why you would be good at it and why the airline you are applying to should employ you and not the next candidate. And remember to make that enthusiasm shine through in every answer.

Interview Tip - Research your Airline

Before you go to your interview try to do a little research into the financial workings of the airline industry and how your particular potential employer makes its money. Airlines are now looking for some degree of business awareness in their new pilots and if you can show you have some knowledge of the financial side of flying it might just give you an edge. For example, what are an airline's biggest costs - (fuel, staff and aircraft). So when the price of crude oil goes up, even just a little, you will see airlines taking a hit in profits.

You should also get hold of a copy of the British Airways annual report as this will detail the previous year's financial performance and give you some valuable background information on the aviation business. Do this regardless of which airline is interviewing you - obviously try an get hold of the annual report for the company that *is* interviewing you as well. In the larger airlines this information is usually available (free) from the company secretary's office. If the receptionist does not appear to understand what you are talking about just ask for someone who can you send the annual report and accounts.

Once you have got it read the chairman's statement and the text at the front, and have a quick look at the graphs, pie charts etc. If there are no graphs and no summary figures right at the front you know it has been a bad year. There is absolutely no point trying to memorise masses of figures. Out of all the financial information available make sure you know the turnover, profit, overall load factor (see below) and perhaps the number of staff employed, and know what the key financial issues facing your potential employer are at the current time.

The other key thing airlines worry about is load factors, or to you and me how many of the seats on each plane have they sold. During 1996 British Airways managed an overall load factor of 73.1%. However, if you could increase this to say 80% without massive discounting of tickets the effect on profits would be dramatic. It effectively costs the same to fly a half empty plane as it does a full one, but the latter will earn you twice as much revenue and a great deal more profit.

Remember also that scheduled airlines make far more money per square ft of floor space on the aircraft out of First and Business Class travel than they do out of Economy. Hence the multitude of frequent flyer programmes aimed at keeping and rewarding those highly lucrative business travellers.

Last of all keep an eye open in the press for new code sharing arrangements / mergers between the airlines. At the time of writing BA is trying to a deal with American Airlines but is running into problems with the European Commission over unfair competition rules on account of the merged airline being too big. Make sure you know how this one turns out as it is bound to be a big talking point at any airline.

Flight International produce an excellent annual survey of the performance and profits of the major international airlines, and this is well worth a read prior to any interviews. The last one was published on 30th July 1997.

The Questions You Should Be Asking Them

Interviews should be a two way process and are normally a good opportunity for you to find out as much as possible about the job, the training and the company. So don't be afraid to ask any questions that you have. Even if you haven't got any burning issues to discuss with your interviewer - they may well have answered all the points you were going to raise already - still ask a couple of questions merely to demonstrate your interest and enthusiasm. The following might give you some ideas.

When will the training programme begin for successful applicants?

How long does training take?

Where does training take place?

Is there any accommodation at the flying school?

Am I guaranteed employment with Snappy Airlines if I pass the training programme?

What is the most challenging part of the training?

What is the average age of pilots at Snappy? *(This is useful to know but be careful how you phrase it especially if your interviewer seems like a very serious chap).*

What type of aircraft would I be most likely to start flying professionally for Snappy?

Do you have any plans to expand your route network?

Would it be possible to be based overseas after a certain period?

What percentage of last year's recruits successfully passed the training programme? *(Again, this is very useful to know but be careful how you phrase it).*

What percentage of those who passed the training programme last year were offered jobs on qualifying? *(Be careful again how you phrase it but this is useful to know).*

Interview Dress

Airlines like their pilots to be conservative, with a small c. Conservative people fit in, follow the rules and are, in the airlines' opinion, less likely to re-design the arrivals lounge with the back end of their aircraft. So when you go to the interview wear something along the lines of a dark blue / black suit, white shirt and a plain tie with black well-polished shoes. Green and brown suits are out and try to avoid the snappy shoes. Donald Duck ties will add little to your application, so leave him in the wardrobe and forget the beard. Women in a sense have more lee-way as there isn't such an established dress code for female pilots, so just make sure you look smart and business-like as you would for any job interview - but conservative with colours, make-up, jewellery etc.

Personality Questionnaires

You are almost certainly going to be asked to fill in what is effectively a personality questionnaire at some point during the assessment process. There are no right or wrong answers, *usually,* but some answers tend to be more right than others. The assessors will be looking for patterns in these questionnaires so really the only good advice I can give is to answer them with 100% honesty and don't think too hard about any one answer.

Unfortunately for you the modern tests have become a great deal more sophisticated and they now have a series of 'control' questions designed to assess how honestly you are answering. For example, the question might say, *have you ever told a lie?* The only answer you can really give is yes because unless you are a saint the chances are everyone will, at some stage during their lives, have told a lie. So if you answer no the computer reading your answer sheet is going to smell a rat. There will be several questions like this and you won't know which they are. However, keep a sharp look out for any question containing the words 'ever' or 'never', as they may well be part of the control set.

The computer will also be looking for consistency in your answers. You will find if you look closely through the questions (which you won't have time to do) that many of them are asking the same thing in different words or exactly the opposite question to one that you have already answered. Unless you have an excellent memory (equal to that of the computer marking your test) you will rapidly discover that if you start lying you will forget what questions you lied about and your test will end up with a high inconsistency score. The next stop for your test and your application form will be the bin - so don't lie!

It is also worth saying that the personality questionnaire can help you as much as the assessors. If you are really not cut out for the left hand seat of a 757 (the captain sits on the left) it is better to find out now than on a windy night trying to land two hundred people at

Tenerife airport when you go to pieces and put half the plane through the airport restaurant!

Anyway, that said I will give you a few examples of the type of thing you'll find in the personality questionnaires just so that you know what to expect.

Do you prefer to work in a group or on your own?

When did you first realise you were interested in flying?

Have you visited any airshows recently?

Did you ever find yourself at odds with teachers when you were at school?

Do you find it easy to make up your mind?

Does anyone in your family fly?

Do you find it hard to motivate yourself when working alone?

Do you like to get home before it gets too late?

Do you like to weigh up all the options before reaching a decision?

When would you say is the best time of your life? Now, in the past or in the future?

Do you often get depressed?

Do you think things aren't as good as they used to be?

Do you ever find you cannot remember what people said to you?

Do people ever talk to you but you miss what they say?

Do you find it difficult to work if there is background noise?

Do you make decisions quickly?

Have you ever driven through an amber traffic light?

Do you ever find you cannot decide whether to stop at amber light before it becomes red?

Do you enjoy staying up all night?

Would you say you were decisive?

Group Exercises

Group exercises are now a popular way for employers to try to find out whether or not you have some of the people skills that they are looking for in their new recruits. Take another look at the list of skills and qualities that airlines are looking for in potential pilots. Several of these such as communication skills, ability to work as a team, critical thinking and leadership potential can all be assessed through the group exercise. The key to group exercises is to shine, but not too brightly. By this I mean join in but don't try to dominate everything. Do your best to make sensible, constructive, suggestions and lead the group if it appears to be lacking direction or firm goals. However, you also need to listen to what the other candidates have to say, and if necessary accept that one of their ideas is more likely to work than yours. Try also to be as positive as possible, even when you are in effect disagreeing with someone.

Frequently group exercises centre around trying to solve some kind of problem - making something for example. These are a good way to assess how well you work with other people so try as much as possible to build on each other's ideas to arrive at the final practical solution.

There is no need to attempt to dominate the conversation or shout the loudest, but at the same time make a contribution. It does no harm either to ask the rest of the group to explain something to you if you don't understand as this will demonstrate that a) you are not arrogant and you don't believe you know everything and b) you are confident enough in a group situation to admit that you don't understand something. Don't be afraid to question the assumptions of others or even of the information you have been given as this will help you to demonstrate critical thinking in a group situation.

To sum up, the group exercise is an important part of the selection process, so treat it seriously. Try to think how you can demonstrate to the assessors some of the core aptitudes that they are likely to be looking for, but at the same time be yourself as there is little point in trying to pretend to be someone you are not. So just as with the interview, application form and personality questionnaire put on your most positive side, but be honest - and try to enjoy it as some of them can be quite good fun!

Is a University Degree a Significant Advantage?

If you are currently considering whether or not to go to university and you are between the ages of 16-21 say, then there are several good reasons for obtaining a degree:

- should you ever for some reason not be able or not want to pursue flying as a career you will find it much easier to go into another well paid career if you have a degree;

- although no airline currently requires a degree as a minimum requirement for pilot training there is no guarantee that they won't change this in the future now that a far higher percentage of school leavers go on to further education;

- a university degree will help distinguish you a little from other less well educated candidates;

- a degree should help you show your potential employer that you are self motivated and can study for and pass written exams;

- you can get some free flying training through a university air squadron while you are there;

- you will have more time to consider your career plans and make up your mind that airline flying is really for you;

- if you study a science based subject - aeronautical / mechanical / chemical / electrical engineering, maths, physics, chemistry or similar you will find flying exams relatively easy in terms of their intellectual level (it is the quantity of information that you must remember that is the hard part);

- most people enjoy university and at the same time you could get a degree in something marketable (e.g. sciences or a vocation - law etc), have some free flying lessons through the university air squadron and then apply for pilot training schemes - at age 22 say.

However, a degree is not the be all and end all of everything, especially if you are older and have not got one. If you are now aged say 25 and did not go to university I would not recommend going now simply to make yourself more marketable to airlines. For one thing you will be reaching the upper age limits by the time you graduate and it is unlikely to make that much difference as you become older. It will be of much greater importance what you have done since leaving school and whether or not you demonstrate the necessary skills and abilities.

Similarly, if you are currently aged about 18, desperate to fly for an airline and always have been and really don't feel that you want to go to university, then why not try for a place on an airline scheme now? If you are successful and you are sure that is what you want to do then great - go ahead and do it - and you'll probably do just fine without a degree. There is no point in going to university if you hate the whole idea and can't think of any subject you want to study as you will probably drop out after a year and that will not look good on your CV. But remember you will be running a higher risk if you are without a degree and things go wrong for some reason with your flying career at a later date.

One last point that I should mention whilst discussing the pros and cons of university is that whilst airlines may be advertising for trainee pilots today there is no guarantee that they will be in three or four years time when you graduate. This is a risk you run of going to college first.

So really the university question depends on how certain you are of what career path you want to take, how academic you are (is there something you would like to study at university?), whether or not you like the idea of going to university and whether you are confident that there will be airline jobs available when you graduate.

Is Having a Private Pilots Licence a Major Advantage?

British Airways say that a PPL or training towards it is **not** a necessary requirement for selection for interviews / aptitude tests. Therefore the selection process is open to all of those who think they may be interested in a career as a professional pilot assuming they meet the other (not too onerous) criteria. However, it is only reasonable to assume they will be looking for evidence of a genuine interest in flying and the aviation business, and therefore some flying experience as a pilot may help you convince them at interviews that you are serious. It could also be argued that it is more reasonable to expect a 25 year old candidate to have demonstrated his or her interest in flying already than an 18 year old school leaver who may not have been able to afford any lessons.

I understand from British Airways that a number of last year's successful applicants had either PPLs or training towards them, but by no means all. For the British Midland scheme they say and I quote:

'The courses are designed for students with no previous flying experience, but candidates for selection will be required to produce evidence of an interest in aviation and some previous flying experience may be an advantage.'

Don't let this put you off applying though, especially for the British Airways scheme as if they really wanted people with flying experience they would ask for it. It is almost certainly more important that you can demonstrate the key skills and interests that I have outlined already.

Women As Pilots

Historically there have been very few women pilots, but this is now changing fast. The airlines are very keen to recruit women into flying roles and they have all looked very closely at their recruitment and selection procedures to ensure that no one category of applicant is at any disadvantage. Some of the majors have also examined how they market themselves to potential employees, and in particular women and ethnic minorities in order to try to encourage more applications from these groups. There has probably never been a better time to become an airline pilot if you are from one of these groups as attitudes have changed a great deal, and will almost certainly continue to do so. However, don't expect positive discrimination either, as equality is now the name of the game.

Age

Generally the age range for most airline schemes tends to be 18-25 or 18-30 or just under when you start training. The best age to be is within the range 21-28. By 21 you have matured a little and are probably more certain of your goals (and hopefully will have got a university degree), and up until your late twenties you should still have at least 25 years flying life left in you. That should be long enough for your employer to get their money's worth. Age is not as critical with the airlines as in the services; the type of flying you will do is quite different and a bit of maturity and experience does no harm.

If you are changing careers it is fair to say that it starts to become significantly more difficult to obtain your *first* flying job once you are in your late thirties (assuming you have paid for all the training yourself), and obtaining sponsorship may well prove impossible. However, there are quite a few ex-military pilots joining the airlines once in their thirties, so if you are determined you may be able to open up an opportunity.

Motivation

It is very likely that during any sponsorship selection process your assessors will be looking not only for evidence of a high level of motivation in your extra-curricular activities, whatever they may be, but also some signs that you are genuinely motivated to becoming a pilot. One way of looking at this is to say if *you* were about to invest £ 60,000 training someone from scratch to do a particular job what attributes would *you* be looking for in candidates? Somewhere in your list of priorities has to be evidence that the candidate is sufficiently committed and motivated to overcome all the hurdles which he or she will face during the training period. In addition you would be hoping to find some indicators that he or she will be both good at and enjoy the job once qualified, meaning your new employee in whom you have invested so much money will be a long term asset to the company. Give these points some thought prior to an interview.

How can I demonstrate Motivation?

University or School Air Squadron / Combined Cadet Force (CCF)

Naturally if your school or university has a CCF (Combined Cadet Force) section with access to RAF flying this is an excellent opportunity to get some hands-on flying experience at very low or zero cost. This could help demonstrate in an interview with any potential airline or military sponsor that you are serious about flying as a career and have tried it out. After all, some people who have never flown as a pilot before have one lesson and find that they don't enjoy it as much as they thought they would, even though they enjoy flying as a passenger.

Other ways of demonstrating an interest in flying...

Gliding

Flying lessons in powered planes may well be out of reach to many younger applicants on cost grounds but glider clubs can be a good way of getting started. Launches usually cost less than five pounds and hiring a glider is a fraction of the cost a plane whilst the instruction is usually free. You can find out where your nearest club is by contacting the British Gliding Association on 01162 531051.

Airfields and Air Traffic Control

Many smaller airfields are happy to receive visitors who want to look around, watch the planes and maybe visit the control tower. It is best to phone in advance, especially if you want to have a look in the control tower, and try to pick a time when they will not be too busy as they will be able to explain more of what they are doing. Weekdays are probably better than weekends as small airfields are swamped with recreational aircraft at weekends. Make sure it's good weather too, otherwise you won't be able to see much. If there is low cloud there won't be much activity either.

Part 3

Alternatives to Sponsorship

Join the Military

An alternative to sponsorship by an airline is to join the military and earn your wings that way. The competition is fierce and selection standards are very high, which is understandable seeing as you may well end up flying very low and very fast in a war zone! However, if you meet the tough selection criteria you could land a job flying a Tornado after a few years.

What's more they pay you rather than the other way round, which makes a refreshing change. You will also find military flying very different, some would say more exciting, than conventional passenger jet aircraft.

There are some major disadvantages though. You will have to sign up for at least 12 years of service and be prepared for the fact that ultimately you are there to fight wars and maybe kill people (remember Vietnam). The services have their own rules and are really a way of life rather than a job, and you need to be able to take orders! So this option doesn't suit everybody.

You may also lose relative seniority if and when you eventually join an airline as many operate seniority systems which are related to length of service. Basically, you are more senior to the pilots that joined after you and it therefore follows that you are junior to the ones that joined before you. This can be very annoying if you move jobs often, but it does reward loyalty. So if you join an airline after training in the military you may find some younger pilots are effectively senior to you. Seniority can affect all sorts of things from what choice of routes you get to who gets the steak for dinner (the crew must eat different meals in case of food poisoning). However, this is still a great deal better than no flying job at all!

Given that military aircraft are so different from civilian airliners it goes without saying that when you leave the military you will still require some quite expensive cross-training in order to be able to fly for an airline. In the past ex-military personnel have used their severance packages and paid leave to pay for this training, thereby gaining their ATPL (airline-transport pilot's licence) and IR (instrument rating), and there is no guarantee of course of obtaining a job. But with a military background you should have mastered the core skills and know how to work towards exams, which should make the conversion process easier.

One other point on a less positive note is that in recent years significant budget cuts in the services have resulted in some pilots doing very little flying. How bad the situation is seems to vary depending on the type of aircraft and which service you are in, but it is perhaps something to be aware of.

So let's have a quick look at each of the services in turn to see what they offer.

The Royal Air Force

In order to be considered for the RAF as a pilot you need to be between 17 and 23 years 11 months when you start training. If you are willing to consider being a navigator then the age limit is 25 years 11 months. You will need at least 5 GCSEs including English and Maths, plus two 'A' levels - sciences preferred, and you will also find having a degree is now a significant advantage.

The RAF has the largest number and variety of aircraft out of the three sections of the services, from Tornado jets to Sea King Helicopters. Initially you will spend your time doing flight training exercises, and then after about three years you would join a squadron in 'front line' roles.

You should be able to keep flying for quite a number of years but you will find that as you get older and more senior the opportunities to fly decrease. It is possible to sacrifice promotion to continue flying though. The availability of flying jobs will also depend on the current state of budget cuts in the Armed Forces.

If you are at or thinking about going to university then joining a university Air Squadron can be a good move. You should have the opportunity to complete a number of flying hours free, and this will give you some idea as to whether you might enjoy a career as a pilot. You don't have to commit yourself either to the RAF.

If you do want to commit yourself to the RAF prior to university then a cadetship might be a good idea. If you are successful in applying the RAF will pay you to go to university and teach you to fly.

The RAF also offer flying scholarships with no commitment whereby you are given 20 hours of free flying and this is particularly suitable for people at school or college.

The recruitment department at RAF Cranwell will be able to give you more details on all of these schemes and the RAF in general on 01400 261201.

The Army Air Corps

The Army principally operates Lynx and Gazelle helicopters, and generally recruits most of its pilots internally from within the Army. So the chances are you would have to join the mainstream army first and then transfer to the Air Corps. This seems rather a long winded and uncertain route to becoming an airline pilot, but if you have some flying experience and think you might enjoy a spell in the Army then applying for one of the small number of direct entry pilot places might be good idea.

Also bear in mind that airlines usually use fixed wing planes, not helicopters, although it could be possible to obtain a job with one of the big helicopter operators such as Bristow once you have left the Army.

Your local Army careers office should be able to give you more information and they can be found in Yellow Pages under Armed Services.

The Royal Navy Fleet Air Arm

The Navy operates Sea Harriers as well as Lynx, Sea King and the new Merlin helicopters, and can offer some very challenging flying. The entry requirements are not quite as strict as the RAF and you can be up to 26 years old when you join as aircrew, but the academic requirements are similar and a degree may well help you get in.

In common with the RAF the Navy offers cadetships for those willing to commit to the service who want to go to university first. They also offer some scholarships and free gliding worth £ 250.

More information on The Royal Navy Fleet Air Arm can be obtained from the Flying Scholarships Officer on 01705 727753.

The Self-Improver Route

The self-improver route basically means getting your PPL and then building your flying experience obtaining IMC, IR and 700 hours flying experience as an instructor or general aviator all at your own cost. This could easily cost you in the region of £ 35,000, and of course there is no guarantee of a job at the end of it. Many people go abroad where the flying is cheaper in order to build their hours, particularly the United States. Obviously you will then need to take your Civil Aviation Authority Licence exam in the UK.

The chances are that unless you own an oilfield or marry an heiress you will need a second (or first - depending on how you look at it) career to finance this route - and one that pays you decent money as well. So my advice is concentrate at least initially on trying to get onto a sponsored pilot training scheme. Not only will it save you a lot of time and money, but also if you have been trained by a reputable airline the chances are you will be much more employable should you ever need another job than if you had just paid for training yourself. You will also find you are led almost by the hand though the maze of exams, experience, type ratings etc. which, although there is no question you will have to work very hard for your new employer, it will be one hell of a lot easier than trying to organise and pay for it all yourself.

Will I Enjoy a Career as a Commercial Airline Pilot?

You will by now have some idea of the qualities required to make a good airline pilot, and the entry qualifications that the airlines look for, as well as a few tips on how to get a head start on the other candidates that you will be competing against.

In a sense, if you have to ask yourself whether you will enjoy flying as a professional career then perhaps you are not right for the job. After all there are many people who have always known that flying was all they ever wanted to do. However, personally I believe it does no harm to give some serious consideration to all the pluses and minuses of flying as a career before you spend a great deal of time and possibly money pursuing your goal. I also believe that if you have got your ambitions clear in your own mind you will also find it a great deal easier to convince a potential employer that you are the right man or woman for their airline sponsorship / training scheme.

So, on the plus side you have:

- the pure fun and enjoyment of flying an aircraft;

- working as a team with like minded colleagues;

- technical and mental stimulation;

- variety in terms of aircraft, weather, routes, changing technology, people;

- opportunity to see the world;

- a well respected professional career;

- seen by others to be an 'interesting' job;

- carrying out a useful social function i.e. transporting people and goods;

- opportunity to meet lots of pretty air hostesses!

- gaining a recognised qualification.

On the minus side you have:

- the need to study and learn a large amount of sometimes tedious information in order to gain the necessary licences;

- the uncertainties of the airline pilot job market - aviation is a very cyclical business and there is no guarantee that you will be employed however much experience you have;

- the risk of losing your licence for one reason or another - although you can insure against this;

- you may have an unsettled home-life with a significant amount of time spent abroad;

- you must be happy being constantly assessed and having your performance checked;

- you must be happy working to very regimented and organised systems and procedures;

- you must be very self-critical and willing to accept criticism from others.

There is no doubt in my mind that the positive aspects far out-weigh the negatives, and the last three negative points are not necessarily disadvantages at all. But these points may well come up during the selection process and it will help you to have considered them thoroughly not only for your potential employer's benefit, but also for your own.

The Future

Predicting what will happen in the future is always a dangerous occupation, but I expect things to change significantly in the next decade in the field of pilot recruitment, and so I have outlined here how I hope things will go.

You will have gathered by now having read this guide that the job market for pilots seeking employment has improved considerably, and that this has led to airlines, large and small, running sponsorship schemes to train new pilots.

However, many of these schemes require candidates to put up sometimes substantial amounts of money, and to guarantee to pay back all training costs if they fail to complete the training programme or a specified period of bonded employment. These requirements are unquestionably onerous, and I suspect a great many potential candidates cannot meet them. Even if candidates can raise the initial cash sum, many may feel unhappy about the parental guarantee, which if things go wrong, could be very serious for the guarantors especially if they are not that wealthy.

As a result of this, pilot training is in effect being rationed in some instances (not all) to those who can afford it, rather than to those who would make the best pilots. I expect this to be a transitionary stage, and in the future, hopefully not too far away, more schemes will be run like the British Airways and SAA schemes which do not disadvantage those from less well off backgrounds.

Similar changes have happened already in other professions, e.g. accountancy where firms' investment in training adds up to over £ 100,000 per individual over three years, which is considerably more than the cost of pilot training. Candidates are not expected to pay for any of this training themselves, and nor do they have to pay any money back if they fail to complete the course. However, I do accept that there is a slight difference in that the costs of flight training are entirely front loaded, and therefore a huge investment must be made in the individual before he or she earns a penny for his or her employer. This does not apply to the same extent in other professions. Nonetheless, I feel it is more appropriate for corporations rather than individuals to be taking this investment risk in training, and this is the attitude that the majors are already taking.

Of course this assumes that we do not enter another recession in the aviation business in the near future, and that predictions of increasing passenger traffic are realised, thereby sustaining the demand for new pilots.

Some employers may argue that so long as there are far more people wanting to be pilots than there are training places available the current system will continue. Whilst that is a possibility, I believe that sustained increases in air traffic will result in a demand by the public and operators alike to reduce the number of accidents that are pilot related. One way to do this is to improve still further the training and competence of our airline pilots. A means of achieving this would be the introduction of more airline run ab initio schemes, selecting only the best and most able candidates and investing heavily in their training, whilst not ruling out a large number of potential applicants on financial grounds.

At the same time I believe self - sponsorship (not in conjunction with any employer) would become a thing of the past, as such people have, on average, been of a slightly lower overall level of ability than those selected through a rigorous airline or military selection process. This is reflected in the fact that those who have been trained by a major airline are generally more employable than those who paid for their own training.

In addition, once the JAA European licence comes into force in 1999 self-improver candidates will have to take modular training courses at approved colleges instead of waiting to log up 700 hours of flying time to gain their CPL. However, 200 hours of approved training will then be sufficient. Overall I believe these changes should make flying training more structured and in the end result in pilots being trained to a higher standard.

I therefore believe that the future for any young man or woman hoping to pursue a career as an airline pilot is very bright. With determination and ability your goal should be within your reach. However, make sure you are prepared to overcome the obstacles that you will doubtless encounter on the way, and don't give up.

All that is left for me to say now is I hope you have found this guide useful and informative, and best of luck in your professional flying career.

Airline Addresses

Air 2000   01293 518966
First Choice House, London Road, Crawley,
West Sussex, RH10 2GX

Air Atlantique   01203 307566
Hangar 5, Coventry Airport, Bagington, Coventry, CV8 3AZ

Air Bristol   01279 680909
Enterprise House, London Stansted Airport, Stansted, Essex,
CM24 1QW

Air Foyle   01582 419792
Halycon House, Luton Airport, Luton, Bedfordshire, LU2 9LU

Air France   00 33 141 567800
45 Rue de Paris, Roissy Charles de Gaulle Cedex, Paris, 95747

Air Kilroe   0161 436 2055
Airside, A Pier, Terminal 1, Manchester Airport, Manchester
M90 3PF

Air New Zealand   00 64 93 66 2400
Quay Tower, Private Bag, 92007, Auckland 1, New Zealand

Air South West   01392 446111
Exeter Airport, Exeter, Devon, EX5 2BD

Airtours International   0161 232 6600
Parkway 3, Parkway Business Centre, 300 Princess Road, Manchester,
M14 7QU

Air UK   01279 660400
Stansted House, Stansted Airport, Stansted, Essex, CM24 1AE

Air UK Leisure   01279 680737
Airways House, First Avenue, Stansted Airport, Stansted,
Essex, CM24 1RY

Airworld   0181 325 3200
25 Elmfield Road, Bromley, Kent, BR1 1LT

American Airlines   001 817 963 1234
4333 Amon Carter Boulevard, Fort Worth (Dallas), Texas, 76155, USA

Aurigny Air Services   01481 66444
States Airport, La Planque Lane, Forest, Guernsey, Channel Islands

Britannia Airways   01582 458594
Luton Airport, Luton, Bedfordshire, LU2 9ND

British Airways
Recruitment & Selections, Meadowbank, S571, 680 Bath Road,
Hounslow, Middlesex, TW5 9QX
Recruitment Recorded Message Line   0181 564 1450
Flight Ops Recruitment including Pilots   0181 564 1422
Graduate Recruitment   0181 564 1367
Switchboard   0181 759 5511

British Midland   01332 854000
Donington Hall, Castle Donington, Derbyshire, DE74 2SB

British World Airlines   01702 354435
Viscount House, Southend Airport, Essex, SS2 6YL

Brymon Airways   01752 705151
City Airport, Crownhill, Plymouth, Devon, PL6 8BW

Business Air   01224 725566
Kirkhill Business House, Howemoss Fr., Kirchhill Ind Estate,
Dyce, Aberdeen, AB2 0GL

Caledonian Airways   01293 668280
Caledonian House, Gatwick Airport, Crawley, West Sussex, RH6 0LF

Cathay Pacific   00 852 27 472888
Swire House, 9 Connaught Road Central, Hong Kong or
Manpower Resourcing Office, Personnel Department, 4th Floor, Block A,
City A Building, Hong Kong International Airport, Hong Kong

Channel Express   01202 593344
Building 470, Bournemouth Int Airport, Christchurch,
Dorset, BH23 6DL

CityFlyer Express   01293 567837
Iain Stuart Centre, Gatwick Airport, West Sussex, RH6 0PB

Easyjet   01582 443355
Easyland, Luton Airport, Bedfordshire LU2 9LS

Emerald Airways   0151 448 0844
South Terminal, Speke Hall Avenue, Liverpool Airport,
Liverpool, L24 1YD

European Aviation Air Charter   01202 581111
European House, Bournemouth Int Airport, Christchurch,
Dorset, BH23 6EA

Flightline   01702 543000
Aviation Way, Southend Airport, Southend, Essex, SS2 6UN

GB Airways   01293 664239
Iain Stuart Centre, Beehive Ring Road South, Gatwick Airport
West Sussex, RH6 0PB

Gill Airways   0191 286 9665
Newcastle Int Airport, Newcastle, Northumberland, NE13 8BL

HeavyLift Cargo Airlines   01279 680611
Stansted Airport, Stansted, Essex, CM24 1QP

Hunting Cargo Airlines   01332 810081
East Midlands Airport, Castle Donington, Derbyshire, DE74 2SA

Iberia   00 34 1587 4747
Calle Velazquez 130, Madrid, E-28006, Spain

Interline   01603 489265
Suite 5, Airport Business Centre, Norwich Airport, Norwich NR6 6BS

Japan Airlines   00 81 354 60 3109
JAL Building, 4-11 Higashi Shinagawa 2 chome, Shinagawa-ku, Tokoyo,
140, Japan

Jersey European Airway   01392 366669
Exeter Airport, Exeter, Devon, EX5 2BD

KLM Royal Dutch Airlines   00 31 20 649 9123
External Communications, (AMS/DR) PO Box 7700, Schiphol
Airport (East), 11172L, Holland.

Lufthansa   00 49 221 8260
                                                  00 49 421 55920
Von Gablenz Strasse 2-6, Cologne, D-50679, Germany

Lufthansa Flight Training GmbH   00 49 421 5592 460 or 461
Pilot School, BRE OT/M, POB 28 61 36, Flughafendamm 40,
D-28361, Bremen, Germany

Loganair   0141 889 1311
St. Andrews Drive, Glasgow Abbotsinch Airport, Paisley,
Renfrewshire, PA3 2TG

Maersk Air   0121 743 9090
2245-49 Coventry Road, Birmingham, B26 3NG

Manx Airlines   01624 826000
Isle of Man Airport, Ballasalla, Isle of Man IM9 2JE

Monarch Airlines   01582 400000
Luton Airport, Luton, Bedfordshire, LU2 9NU

Northwest Airlines   001 612 726 2331
5101 Northwest Drive, St Paul, Minnesota, 55111-3034, USA

Qantas Airways   00 61 2 9691 3636
Qantas Centre, 203 Coward St, Sydney, NSW, 2020, Australia

Ryanair UK   01279 663082
Room 610, Terminal Building, Stansted Airport, Stansted, Essex

SAS Scandinavian Airlines   00 46 87 97 0000
Frosundaviks Alle 1, Stockholm, S-16187, Sweden

Sabre Airways   01293 410727
12 The Merlin Centre, County Oak Way, Crawley,
West Sussex, RH11 7XA

Singapore Airlines   00 65 542 3333
Airline House, 25 Airline Road, 819829, Singapore

South African Airways   00 27 11 978 5161
Office of the Executive Manager, Human Resources,
Private Bag X13, Room 304E, Airways Park, Johannesburg International
Airport, 1627, South Africa

Streamline Aviation   01392 360424
Exeter Airport, Exeter, Devon, EX5 2BD

Suckling Airways   01223 292525
Cambridge Airport, Newmarket Road, Cambridge, CB5 8RT

Titan Airways   01279 680616
Enterprise House, Stansted Airport, Stansted, Essex, CM24 1QW

TNT International Aviation Services   01753 842168
Archway House, 114-116 St Leonards Road, Windsor,
Berks, SL4 3DG

United Airlines   001 847 700 4000
Jobline   001 888 825 5627
PO Box 66100, Chicago, Illinois, 60660, USA

United Parcel Service Airlines (UPS)   001 502 329 6500
1400 North Hurstbourne Parkway, Louisville, Kentucky, 40223, USA

Virgin Atlantic Airways   01293 562345
Ashdown House, 2nd Floor, High Street, Crawley,
West Sussex, RH10 1DG

Glossary of Terms

Ab initio
General term referring to flying courses or sponsorship schemes which start from first principles and assume no previous flying experience or knowledge as a pilot.

ATPL
Air Transport Pilot's Licence - this allows you to fly as the Captain of any airliner for which you are type rated..

BCPL
Basic Commercial Pilot's Licence - this allows you to work as a paid PPL flying instructor within certain parameters. Requires a minimum of 200 hours flying time but under the JAR this rating is due to be outmoded. Allows a pilot to fly for reward on non-passenger carrying flights.

CAA
Civil Aviation Authority.

CPL
Commercial Pilot's Licence. This allows a pilot to fly passengers for reward. Currently requires either 200 hours approved training or 700 hours self-improver in addition to ground exams and a flight test.

FAA
Federal Aviation Authority (USA).

ATPL(frozen)
Where a student has completed the necessary written exams for the ATPL but needs to build up flying hours. Once this is done the ATPL can be 'unfrozen' and the student will then have gained the ATPL. To defrost your ATPL you will need 1500 hours of flying experience.

IFR
Instrument Flight Rules.

IMC
Instrument Meteorological Conditions (i.e. weather below VMC standard). IMC is also a rating which can be added to the basic licence allowing you to fly in poorer weather.

IR
Instrument Rating. This is an additional rating to the PPL or CPL licence which allows you to fly in controlled airspace and bad weather under Instrument Flight Rules.

JAA
The Joint Aviation Authorities, which are helping to harmonise European aviation regulations.

JAR
The Joint Aviation Requirements. These are to be implemented across Europe in 1999 thereby harmonising aviation licences.

Multi-Engine Rating
Allows a pilot to fly an aircraft with more than 1 engine.

Night Rating
Allows a pilot to fly at night.

NVQ
National Vocational Qualification. A Government training initiative. Enables students to claim tax back against training costs. See section on British Midland.

PIC
You took part in a particular flight and you flew as Pilot in Command.

PPL
Private Pilot's Licence. Allows a pilot to fly a single engine aircraft under 5700 kg in daylight and in good weather. Requires 40 hours of flying training, 20 of which must be solo as well as six ground exams, a Class 3 medical and a flight test.

Type Rating
Once you have your ATPL you will need a type rating in order to be able to fly a particular type of aircraft as obviously they are not all identical.

VFR
Visual Flight Rules. These are the rules under which basic PPL holders fly. You must steer clear of controlled airspace, fly in good weather and keep clear of other aircraft.

VMC
Visual Meteorological Conditions. Weather in which visual flight is safe. Pilot should remain in sight of the ground.

Reader Update Service

During 1998 we will be introducing a reader update service. This will contain the latest updated information on current sponsorships and training schemes as well as keeping you informed of developments in the pilot job market.

If you would like to register your interest in this service just send your name and address on a postcard quoting reference 'Reader Updates' to the address below and we will send you more information.

Get That Job! Guides, Reader Updates (Pilots),
6 Latymers,
Penshurst,
Tonbridge,
Kent,
TN11 8DE,
UK

or email GetThatJobGuides@btinternet.com